THE
MYSTERIES
OF
SEDONA

By

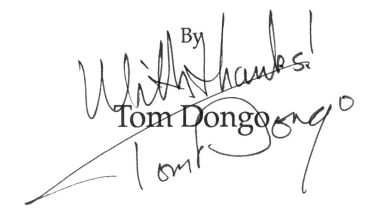

Tom Dongo

All Photos and Artwork by
the author

Published by
Hummingbird Publishing

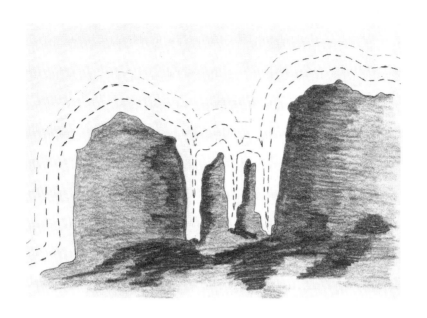

Cathedral Rock

© 1988 by Tom Dongo

ISBN 0-9622748-0-1
Previously ISBN 0-929385-07-1

Published by
Hummingbird Publishing
P.O. Box 2571, Sedona, AZ 86336
For inquiries or orders see page 85.

Printed by
Mission Possible
2020 Contractors Rd. Suite 5
Sedona, AZ 86336

Second edition

Printing 15 14 13 12 11 10 9

TABLE OF CONTENTS

DEDICATION

With special thanks to the many Sedona residents who contributed to this book by their insights, their criticism, their praise - and their valuable time.

Chapel Area

SEDONA

Sedona, Arizona, situated in the heart of the American desert Southwest, is one of the planet's most sacred sites. Here in Sedona is a rapidly growing metaphysical community which has roots stretching to the new age, new thought, communities of the world.

Sedona and neighboring Oak Creek Canyon have long been holy ground for Indian tribes such as the Hopi, Navajo, Apache, Yavapai, and, before them, the Sinagua and Hohokam. It is a crossroads for the evolving New Age Family of Man - as seekers from all points of the U.S. and the world travel to Sedona's beautiful and mysterious red rock mountains, pinnacles and canyons to find their own particular and individual enlightenment.

Sedona has become the recent home to many new, adventurous residents who were irresistibly "drawn" here. Drawn by a magnetic force few understood, but a force few could resist. Each story is surprisingly the same. Typically it is told like this, "I felt such a strong pull to Sedona that after a period of time, Sedona became an obsession. One day the decision was made; I quit my secure job, sold my house, said good-bye to my astonished friends and relatives, and moved two thousand miles to a place I had never seen . . . When I arrived, I felt I had come home!"

Ask a hundred new age immigrants to Sedona and you will hear the same story. Perhaps with slight variations, but the theme is always the same.

Some arrivals find fulfillment and accomplishments beyond their wildest dreams. While others drift away after a time frustrated and disillusioned, never really discovering what they sought. Perhaps because they didn't listen. There is a saying in Sedona that either Sedona treats people wonderfully - or it chews them up and spits them out. Quite true - and there is a very valid underlying reason for it. The type(s) of energy that exist in the Sedona area tend to very quickly bring out the best in people - or the worst.

Its a familiar experience here in Sedona. Whatever a person has within comes directly to the surface and is amplified proportionately. If it is love and compassion - then that person becomes even more loving and caring and quickly finds others who are of the same kind. But if one has suppressed negative emotions - hate, fear, jealousy, judgment, etc., that also comes right to the surface. Either the individual, for various reasons, won't deal with it and retreats - or faces it head on and resolves sometimes very difficult negative patterns, which may otherwise have taken lifetimes to overcome or correct. It's a phenomenon seldom seen anywhere else - not quite like here.

Ask any metaphysical resident who has been in Sedona for a while. They each have lots of stories of their own. In Sedona you have to be careful of what you think - what you have on your mind - because those thoughts INSTANTLY begin to manifest. Whether good for you or bad for you - you learn not to be careless about your thought process.

Because there is a growing amount of literature published on Sedona and what you are likely to find here - and as a result of numerous conversations with visitors and locals alike, I felt there was a real need to present an esoteric side of the picture which perhaps is being avoided by other writers, possibly for fear of ridicule, criticism, ostracism, etc. There are a lot of things going on in Sedona that are perhaps only being superficially touched upon by much of the literature that is available. Maybe this will fill in that gap - or add more fuel to the fire.

I want to point out that most of what you are about to read is not verifiable by established cut-and-dried scientific means. Much of it is in the realm of metaphysical science of the mind - and which will become the greater reality in the future? The majority of the following observations were drawn from my own sources, or were related to me by those whom I felt were responsible and credible individuals. Stories that I felt had no foundation whatsoever I have totally disregarded. However, I have found that the bulk of this information has been validated in one way or another; by odd coincidences, psychics, channels, books - and most of all by metaphysical people from all over the world.

To define Sedona in terms of principles of reality transcending those of any particular science, metaphysics, one could say that it is a town situated in a vast zone of powerful, shifting, mysterious and sometimes volatile energies. To label these energies in only magnetic or electromagnetic terms is to restrict their greater meaning. These energies are truly cosmic and of many variations and applications. Energy emits from the earth in the deserts, mesas and canyons in and around Sedona. Certain energies (vortexes) are at the moment in specific locations but can appear occasionally, or intensify, anywhere in the Sedona area. It is said that somehow Sedona's iron rich red rocks draw or generate these powers. It is said that these energies will soon expand and become one - and then join with other energies and then expand across the face of the earth. And probably so!

SEDONA

The Sedona energy field completely envelops Sedona. If you are one who is sensitive to energies, you can feel the boundaries of this energy while driving in and out of Sedona. It seems to extend roughly in a five to eight-mile radius from the center of the town; with emphasis on the west, northwest, south and southwest.

There are four primary\stationary focuses of Sedona's vibrant energies at this time. They are Bell Rock, Cathedral Rock, Boynton Canyon and the Airport Vortex. They are covered more specifically in Chapter Four.

Timeless Sentinels

CHAPTER ONE

The Entrances of Fay and Boynton Canyon

THE CANYONS

Among the many canyons surrounding Sedona, it is Boynton Canyon where I prefer to spend my time when I am studying and observing energies and non-physical life forms. I have the ability to clairvoyantly see vortexes, or any dense energy form such as a non-physical being, so it is relatively easy for me to locate them after I have made particular psychic adjustments. When I first arrived in Sedona, I found that some of the vortexes I visited and that were marked by Indian Medicine Wheels (rocks arranged in a wagon wheel formation) and were popular visitation spots, actually had no unusual energy at all. In the last year, almost all of these false vortexes have been disregarded by new age people.

Boynton Canyon has at least seven major concentrations of energy. In the more literal sense ALL of Boynton Canyon could be termed a vortex, or better yet, an energy spring. Individually the colors of these power spots are white/blue, blue/green, silver, violet, blue, silver/blue, and light pink. These colors vary in intensity from day to day of whatever shade they are, and will drift out of position at times - sometimes as much as several yards. I would like to stress that the color impression of an energy area is not particularly important.   What is important is the "feel" of a power spot, and how it affects you.

Soldier's Pass

THE CANYONS

Deep in several of the canyons exist unseen beings that for years local residents, ranchers, and psychics alike have called the Rock People. Their mysterious presence has been felt over the years and thus the legend. On one of my hikes I discovered what I think are the Rock People. This was early summer of '87 and the first unexpected encounter was very uneasy for both sides. The first one of these entities I met quickly realized I could actually see him (it) and there was from the entity an emanation of suspicion and unease. It was like trying to find common ground, or making friends, with a wild animal - that is the best way I can describe that first experience. There was a considerable degree of wariness on my part and also on theirs for several months. During this time I often had telepathic callings from them. My impression of them now has changed completely from what it was originally. They, I now know, are intelligent, curious, powerful and even somewhat playful at times.

The Indians knew of them hundreds of years ago, probably thousands of years ago. The Indians called them the Wapeka. Remains of the ruins of Indian cliff dwellings are in evidence in almost all of the canyons. Most of these ruins date back at least seven hundred years. There is archaeological probability that Indian settlements were here as early as 11,000 years ago.

Rock People/Wapeka

THE CANYONS

The ancient Indians developed a close, working relationship with these beings and in turn, the Wapeka entities, being almost devic in their evolution, helped the Indians in growing their crops and to find good water. These beings are energy beings originally from deep space, and if angered through ignorance they can make things most unpleasant by playing on our own fears. This is precisely what has happened on many occasions to unsuspecting hikers who ventured through their home territory. They are especially reactive to those who venture into these areas with anger, and who have destructive, negative/aggressive tendencies in their personalities. The one thing I have found that riles them the most is making changes to their turf, such as clearing brush or cactus, rolling rocks down hillsides, or throwing trash around. (See note 1 at end of chapter.)

In some of the instances which I know of personally where these Wapeka beings (and most certainly others) have made things interesting for humans are as follows:

A woman who was in a hiking group I was with decided to go on ahead after we had stopped. She said she wanted to look at a particular part of a side canyon. Shortly after leaving us, she returned, greatly excited. She explained that at one point she literally came up against an energy force like a wall that would not allow her to advance one step further. She said she distinctly heard a voice cautioning her not to go one step more. She quickly retraced her steps at that point back to the group.

A direct personal experience I had was with a metaphysical group in late summer. We had hiked to a remote vortex for a clairvoyance and meditation session. There were a husband and wife in the group that did not fit in well with the others. In fact, they didn't fit in well with the group, the canyon energies, or the natural surroundings.

After a group meditation, we had all separated from each other to allow ourselves privacy for a personal, individual meditation. I was sitting quietly on a hillside in a brush enclosed clearing when in my mind I heard the words, "We want all of you out of here, NOW!" I wasn't entirely sure that this wasn't coming from my imagination since I was at the time deep in what was a blissfully pleasant meditation. I dutifully acknowledged the suggestion. But at the same time I chose to continue to meditate for a while longer - whether the nebulous voice liked it or not. An uncomfortable feeling was growing in the air. It continued for about ten minutes and then suddenly, to my surprise, it was gone and the energy was back to normal. Pondering all this for a few moments, I decided I had best heed the warning, rejoin the group and leave the area.

As I made my way down to the others, who were already regrouped, I was told, to my added surprise, that the man and wife I described had left ten minutes earlier in a curious rush. They exclaimed, upon leaving, a few hasty words to the effect that they thought it was going to rain. Oddly enough, the sky was clear that day.

In another unusual incident, a party of three men and three women who had just met, and knew nothing of the canyon's strange reputation, were hiking far into Boynton Canyon. The men, who were evidently separated from the women, saw something so frightening that they ran in terror out of the canyon, drove back to their motel, and immediately left Sedona with hardly a word to anyone.

In another strange incident, a well-known local mountain climber and desert hiker said he was followed for a considerable distance in Boynton Canyon by a small, three-foot-tall creature that he said was definitely not human.

In July 1988, as I was finishing the first draft of this book, a paranormal encounter was related to me by a very close friend. She described to me how her 23 year old daughter, vacationing from out of state, and a friend, had witnessed a highly unusual spectacle.

CHAPTER TWO

They had attended a meditation ceremony on Schnebly Hill and were the first to leave. It was after 8:30pm by then and almost totally dark. The pair had started back to their parked car. They were crossing a dry creek bed when a faint blue/white light began to form off to their left.

As they watched, the faint light grew brighter and brighter. Then the light began to very slowly pulse. It would dim to a small spot and then expand again to its peak brightness. This transpired near them for about five minutes. They did not remain to inspect the light further. They talked later of how the blue/white light was of extreme beauty, yet at the same time a bit eerie because they had never seen anything like it before.

Similarly - a man who was hiking in Long Canyon, whose mind was distantly removed thinking about personal matters, suddenly found himself surrounded by a dozen or more brilliant lights of different colors he said were the size of tennis balls.

After the shock wore off, he tried to touch the lights, but they kept just out of reach. He described how they remained with him, sometimes darting about at great speed, for five minutes - then they were gone as quickly as they had appeared.

THE CANYONS

This next episode is different in that I didn't talk to the young woman directly, but indirectly through acquaintances of hers here in Sedona. In the spring of 1987 she was taking a weekend camping holiday from the heat of Phoenix. She had made camp in a remote part of Boynton Canyon - she was well outfitted.

As the story goes, sometime before dark she was sitting in front of a small campfire, when she heard something crashing through the woods behind her that was making some kind of sound that was rather frightening. And she said whatever it was was of enormous size because of limbs breaking, etc. Whatever it was, it instilled so much fright in her that she leaped up and bolted away leaving all of her camping equipment behind and did not return for it.

I do wish she would have turned around and looked before she left. It might have added an interesting piece to a big puzzle. And here again I firmly believe that it is our own fears working against us - and some of these mysterious beings know exactly how to play on those fears.

Sometimes I find myself wondering that if perhaps our ignorance at times is humorous to some of them. And maybe the opportunity to have a little fun just cannot be resisted - a bit like Halloween.

CHAPTER TWO

Everything out there is not always as deadly serious as we think it is.

These occurrences and the ones to follow are some of the incidents I have personally experienced, or were told to me by responsible, intelligent and well grounded individuals. I am sure there are many other stories such as these that I have not heard of.

These incidents are not typical and do not happen to everyone who enjoys a walk in the desert or in the canyons. Perhaps one person in a thousand has experiences this dramatic. I offer them only as an added piece to the Sedona Mystery. Perhaps you have an answer to this great riddle?

As a partial explanation of the more unusual episodes, I have located, in the area of the more bizarre encounters, what I will call an interdimensional portal. This is an area 200 yards in length that beings physical and non-physical "phase" through from time to time. I think this is a crossing point where travellers from countless dimensions intersect and sometimes they pause on their journeys to have a look around on this planet. It is then that these cosmic travellers come into direct contact with hikers, and the chance meeting - for the humans - has predictable results. (See note 2 at end of chapter.)

THE CANYONS

Ships as well as individuals travel these inter-dimensional "highways". In the zone of this particular portal area I saw a type of space being that I considered to be very exotic. I did not feel that it (they) was hostile or dangerous. But as is often the case they did not want to be interfered with in any way. This being communicated to me that desire in precise telepathic terms. I have not since re-encountered this type of being.

CHAPTER TWO

There is also at times in the canyons a mysterious cosmic entity which vaguely resembles an upside-down cyclone. It is a gentle being of enormous power. The being is comfortable to be in the vicinity of, but I believe its energy is not compatible with ours. I am quite certain that if a human were to DELIBERATELY merge with an entity of THIS type, there would be an adverse affect to the human's energy system.

As bizarre as this last sighting sounds, one of those odd coincidences I mentioned at the beginning comes into play here. A month after this sighting I was talking to a woman whom I had just met. She was explaining to me that her extremely psychic sensitive daughter in northern California recently had called her very late one evening. Her daughter said she had just had a vivid vision of a cyclone-like being that was in a canyon a few miles west of Sedona. The description and location matched my experience almost exactly. The girl had never been to Sedona, and until the woman brought it up I had not mentioned the sighting to anyone.

What I have presented could be interpreted as a rather disparaging picture of humanity interacting with these exotic and alien life forms. But it is a side of the coin that must be understood, or at least entertained, now, by the unwary or unaware individual.

CHAPTER TWO

In the strongest of terms, I assure you these beings exist - they are as alive and real as we are! And in the very near future mankind, one way or another, will suddenly find itself in a face to face interaction and communication with these superbeings from space. It is long past the point of "Do they really exist?" Rather of, "Let's find out who they are - and begin to work with them." Sedona is a hotbed of extra-terrestrial activity in all forms.

Most of these visitors, through watchful studies, know far more about us than we do of ourselves. These beings, when encountered, must be interacted with by mature, well grounded thinkers which commands mutual respect by both sides. The meeting must be as residents of equal status in the universe - AND WITH NO HUMAN FEAR. Fear is an emotion that some of them know nothing about - or, it is regarded as a nuisance they would rather not bother with.

I have been told that there is a race of dwarflike beings from deep space called Zeta-Reticuli who are approximately three million years ahead of us. Their evolution did not include fear, and it is very difficult for them to deal with a panic stricken human in a chance meeting. The vibration of fear is extremely harmful to them. They carry a small device the size of a pencil which sedates a human upon activation.

These space beings, and there are hundreds of races of them, have been on this planet as long as we have. It is not an invasion by aliens from outer space as some would like to believe. If they were here to take us over they could have done it eons ago. We have a momentous opportunity, for now, finally, the Family of Man has the OPTION to join the Cosmic Family of the Universe. And these great beings, if we would become less fearful and more open minded (particularly if we would let go of the "shoot first and ask questions later" mentality) would welcome us as sisters and brothers. We have to break free from an entrenched reality of self-enforced limited perceptions and make a non-fear/fantasy effort to understand them and their reality.

THERE IS A CERTAIN "BASE LOGIC" or common sense approach, Which can be applied TO ALL UNIVERSAL AND DIMENSIONAL LIFE FORMS AND EXISTENCES, even though by nature they can be termed infinite and indeed they are.

To end this chapter I would like to mention what I called a cosmic device. It was a silvery color a hundred feet long and ten feet high, near the top of a cliff at the back of Long Canyon.

In the summer of 1987 I attended a channeling session at the then Temple of Light in Sedona.

CHAPTER TWO

During the session, the entity the woman was channeling asked if anyone would like to ask questions on anything of general interest. I quickly took the opportunity to ask about the mysterious device. After a long pause, the spiritual entity she was channeling said he did not have the information, and would stand aside for another who did. In moments, an entity named Korton, who said he was in charge of communications for The Ashtar Space Group, came through. He expressed surprise that I was aware of the device. His explanation was that the device had other applications, but basically it was a communication station for the Ashtar Space Group. Then Korton left and the previous entity returned.

As a continuation of odd coincidences, the following day when the tape was replayed, the entire conversation of the explanation of the device was missing. But conversations before and after were intact and clear. The tape recorder had not been turned off, nor had the tape been removed during the session.

THE CANYONS

Footnote 1 - page 11:

I have been asked quite often if these are inner earth beings and I really don't know. I do know that they easily pass through solid objects, but the whole concept of civilizations that live in a hollowed out earth is one I have difficulty with. Although I can readily accept the theory that there is some kind of a parallel dimension that corresponds in a material connection to our actual physical earth - and that these beings which live in that space somehow utilize the dense matter of our own earth for their evolution in harmony with our own human surface evolution. There is some astounding evidence of this in Admiral Byrd's detailed and vivid account of his flight to the North Pole in 1948 and his unexpected encounter with a super advanced race of humans who seemed to live IN the earth.

Footnote 2 - page 16:

In the area of this portal I hiked with Virgil (Posty) Armstrong, who is a retired Military Intelligence officer and an international UFO lecturer. Virgil travels the globe investigating these types of paranormal phenomena. We went to the focus point of this energy and he remarked to me that he had not experienced an energy source as powerful as that anywhere in the world.

Bell Rock

SEDONA VORTEX SITES

Bell Rock

Bell Rock is the most well known, and certainly the most familiar of the vortexes because of its unusual bell shape and its close proximity to Highway 179, which connects Sedona to Interstate 17. It is by far the most visited of all the vortexes, and perhaps the most famous. Bell Rock is considered to be an energy beacon which attracts UFOs. There have been many UFO sightings in the vicinity of Bell Rock over the years, usually near the top of the mountain. It is here that vortex energy emits into space, and for some reason extra-terrestrials seem to be interested in this energy emission. Bell Rock is also considered by the Yavapai-Apache to be the Sacred Home of the Eagle. Bell Rock is well known for the many almost miraculous physical and mental healings that have occurred on its numerous power spots. These power spots are found all around the base of the mountain. And at the summit of the mountain there is a particularly intense energy concentration.

CHAPTER THREE

Cathedral Rock

Cathedral Rock's energy areas are seldom visited because of their inaccessibility. Cathedral's energy areas are from mid-mountain up to the top. The very top of the mountain is reachable only by rock climbers with ropes. There are no permanent, defined trails on Cathedral Rock and its rocky brush and cactus-covered slopes are difficult to climb.

Cathedral Rock is possibly the most beautiful single spot in Arizona, and the most photographed. Its four towering red rock citadels are magnificent.

Many locals and out-of-town seekers alike now feel that Cathedral Rock is not a vortex, although it does impart very special energies. I tend to agree that it is not a vortex - certainly not in the manner of Airport, Boynton Canyon and Bell Rock. But I think it would be ultimately up to those who are experiencing the mountain's energies to decide. If one is so inclined, the challenging hike to Cathedral's saddle is well worth it, for the panoramic view and lofty spires are very special.

SEDONA VORTEX SITES

Airport Vortex

Airport Vortex is aptly named because it is on the way to the Sedona Airport. It is situated in a small side canyon. It has a main vortex that is long - about 100 feet long and ten feet wide. The vortex has several outlying "hot spot" areas. It is an extremely powerful vortex. For most people it is a pleasant place to find peaceful meditation, contemplation and relaxation with SELF, and the nature and cosmic elements.

Boynton Canyon

Boynton Canyon is a clairvoyant's Horn of Plenty, or Third-Eye Heaven. There is a little bit of everything going on in Boynton Canyon. It is a good place to practice clairvoyance. Everyone has psychic ability and clairvoyance; it is merely a matter of acknowledging it and allowing it to express itself. In the Boynton area Indian past life visions are common; write down your experiences immediately so the essence of the experience is not lost. Psychic impressions are sometimes like dreams - they fade very quickly and the information may later be of utmost importance.

CHAPTER THREE

Secret Canyon

Because of its remoteness I have not yet fully explored Secret Canyon. But I believe in time it will be determined to be the energy/psychic center of Sedona. Secret Canyon is approximately two miles long with towering walls and is an extraordinarily powerful and mysterious place.

Nearly all the vortexes and energy areas are within public lands. Sedona is surrounded by the Coconino National Forest and there are ample pullouts for a car just about any place you wish to stop. But there are sections of private land. Excellent national forest maps are available at the Forest Service Ranger Station on Brewer Road in Sedona. These maps clearly specify what areas are private and which are public. In addition, Sedona vortex maps are now available at many locations in Sedona. These give detailed driving instructions to the vortex areas. Vortex maps are either free or are reasonably priced.

UNDERSTANDING, EXPERIENCING, AND ENJOYING THE VORTEXES

Vortexes, or energy springs, are very magical places. If you are fortunate to be able to spend time in a vortex, spend at least an hour alone - by yourself - in the vortex. If you come with a group, separate from them for a while, for the vortexes are a highly profound personal experience. Group meditation is fine, but to gain the full experience of a vortex - be by yourself for a bit.

There are no good or bad vortexes, they just ARE. Some vortexes feel better than others. Judge for yourself by the feel of a vortex how it can benefit you: trust your perceptions and information. Everyone is affected differently by a particular vortex.

Vortexes ABUNDANTLY intensify spiritual/psychic abilities and desires.

The immediate effect of the more powerful vortexes can often be felt as a a sudden change in air pressure - an electric density. Some express a feeling of buoyancy and some people are physically swayed from side to side by these energies.

Never try to intellectualize the vortex. Don't try to break it down into categories. Instead, join your energies with the vortex and experience the "feeling" of vortex energy. Join yourself in loving appreciation with the wind, the sun, the infinite blue sky, the fragrances of the earth and the rapture of the uncluttered red rock panorama. Allow yourself to be enveloped by the energy, and let yourself be filled even to the cellular level with this balancing vibrational harmony. It is here, in a vortex, that you can integrate what you are in a communion of you, your essence, with Mother Earth nature elements.

It has been said often, that the answers and solutions to the most complicated and long-ranging of life's problems can be found in the divine simplicity of nature. The wind, the flowers, the sun, the rain, the song of a bird - the answers all lie in this wonderment of simplicity. The vortexes magnify greatly our communion with devic/angelic nature elements. And then intensify our communion with the spirituality of simplicity. Meditation. Join in the tranquil peace of vortex energy, and open to the spicy desert wind as it flows through you, and carries with it your personal problems and pains. Give that undesired energy back to the universe to be used in more appropriate ways. Quiet your mind and affirm yourself to be balanced and aligned by these mysterious vortex energies.

If you can't locate a vortex precisely the first time - don't fret about it. Go to the approximate area and let yourself be drawn to a particular spot. That is your spot and it may be far better than the "popular" vortex which might be on the maps, in the books, and in the pamphlets. There are thousands of caves, nooks, shelves, cliffs and overlooks in the Sedona canyons which have special energy that is every bit as beneficial as the established vortexes. I feel that the energies of the Sedona area in general are far more valuable and beneficial when TAKEN IN COMBINATION with the vortex areas. You don't have to be in or on a vortex to experience it. You may find a special place just for you that no one else has ever been to.

Seekers who have experienced vortex energies have had physical and mental healings, contacts with spirit and space entities, past life regression, future visions and other paranormal experiences as diverse as there are personalities. And not uncommonly, space ships and alien beings are sometimes seen in the vicinity of the vortexes.

CHAPTER FOUR

There have been far too many extra-ordinary experiences connected to vortexes to dismiss them, as some would, as something such as a hopeful, ecstatic, or religious mass delusion by overly impressionable individuals.

I will mention here that I think the word "vortex" for these mysterious energy emissions is perhaps not the best terminology. Although because it has become popularized I am sure it will remain "vortex", and I will use the term here and there as a general reference. Sedona vortexes as a rule do not necessarily spin or rotate. Many of them are just there, stationary, radiant, vibrant, glowing, powerful. From my clairvoyant observations I believe the afore mentioned phrase "energy spring" would be more accurate - as they ARE energy springs, just as there are fresh water springs emanating from the Earth. Energy springs are Mother Earth in the purest sense of the word. Coincidentally, Sedona has some of the cleanest, pollution-free air in the world. It is suspected that the vortexes have something to do with it!

If you have crystals or personal stones, bring them and charge them with vortex energy for later use, but do clean the crystals first; discharge them in whatever way you do it. If the crystal is fully charged with some other type of energy when you arrive, it will not be able to absorb vortex energy. It may even release its energy into the vortex. If you have been using crystals for healing, the energy released may be very counteractive to the vortex's energy. All of existence is energy; it is a very volatile and conducive substance.

What many don't realize is that they are inadvertently using the vortexes as a dumping ground. They leave feeling healed and renewed, but their negative energy vibration remains in the vortex field.

One way to alleviate the situation of leaving negative energy (there are many ways) is to ask the divine, white light spirits or your own master guides/teachers to assist in cleansing yourself, your etheric field and the vortex of "bad" energy. It is simple, really, and it works - but so few think of it. You can do this on arrival or on leaving a vortex. One doesn't drink out of a clear mountain spring and then throw garbage in it - a crude analogy, but it is the same thing.

One of the consequences of the vortexes' growing renown is that they are now a general tourist attraction. This can sometimes result in a disruption of the energy of the more easily accessible vortexes by curiosity seekers and picnickers, who have little or no regard for the fragileness and sacredness of the area. (Many power spots are not marked at all.) Cigarette butts, beer cans, candy wrappers, fast food litter, and even toilet paper is sometimes the result, and it causes a noticeable change in the vortex energy. One of these often visited vortexes is a tall monolithic rock, a sacred place the Indians call Changing Woman - it is accessed by hundreds of people a week during the summer. But, like a flowing spring of crystal pure water, the vortexes will cleanse and rejuvenate themselves during periods of little traffic. Fortunately, most who experience them regard the vortexes as a holy shrine - a church - and come with a respect and reverence that keeps the vortexes in the perfect natural condition they should be.

A SCIENTIFIC EXPLANATION OF VORTEXES

Conventional scientific definitions usually categorize vortexes as electro-magnetic, magnetic, psychic, natural, electrical, kinetic, thermal, atomic, gravitational, astrometrical, cosmic, potential, positive, negative, inductive and extrusive.

Vortexes are linear, and extend through the earth. The opposite polarity vortex to Sedona's emerges in the Indian Ocean with the closest land mass being the St. Paul Islands. There is one central Sedona vortex emanation. The other Sedona area offshoot vortexes are spread over a radius of about ten miles. These others are offshoots of the main vortex and they have followed geographic faultlines, or some other irregularity in the earth's surface, and have emerged in their present locations.

World vortex locations and their corresponding opposites, in alphabetical order:

(This information and the following 4 paragraphs are reprinted with permission of the author, Alsgoud Sprinke, from his pamphlet, "An Overview of the Geophysical Aspects of Vortexes." Mr. Sprinke is a geophysicist associated with the world-renowned Institute of Meta/Geophysical Studies.)

"Angkor Watt, Cambodia	Machu Picchu, Peru
Bermuda, Atlantic Ocean	The Stirling Range, Western
. . . .	Australia
City of Refuge, Hawaii	Kalahari Desert, Botswana
Great Pyramids, Egypt	Tubuai Island, South Pacific Ocean
Kathmandu, Nepal	Easter Island, South Pacific Ocean
Mihintale, Sri Lanka	Galapagos Islands, Pacific Ocean
North Geographic Pole	South Geographic Pole
North Magnetic Pole	South Magnetic Pole
Sedona, Arizona	Amsterdam and St Paul Islands,
. . . .	Indian Ocean
Stonehenge, England	Stewart Island, New Zealand
Ulan Ude, USSR	Tierra Del Fuego, Chile

These sites have been located and confirmed by modern technological instruments.

CHAPTER FOUR

"It is well known that the concentrated types of energy that exist at a vortex do affect life forms, including human beings.

"It is interesting to note that ancient civilizations, in a number of cases, seem to have recognized the locations of vortexes and to have been drawn to them. It is generally assumed that these people did not have instruments capable of geo-energy measurement.

"Archaeological data seems to indicate that pre-European civilizations were cognizant of the geo-energy fields existing at this vortex. (Sedona) Numerous settlements and sites of probable religious derivation have been located within the diffusion area, and appear to be concentrated at the diffusion channel exits.

"Twenty-two vortexes, constituting the poles of eleven vortex axes, have been identified worldwide. It is not known whether or not all existing vortexes have been discovered: however, no identifiable pattern seems to exist that might yield any new vortex discovery, and geo-energy measurements appear to indicate that the mapped geo-energy fields of the earth are complete."

A friendly reminder, when you visit vortex areas or other fragile natural sites - have consideration for the land and for others who will follow you in the days, months and years ahead

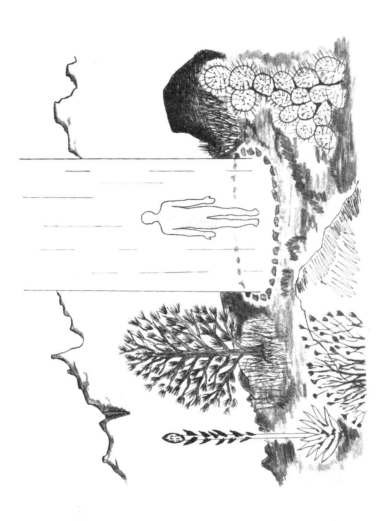

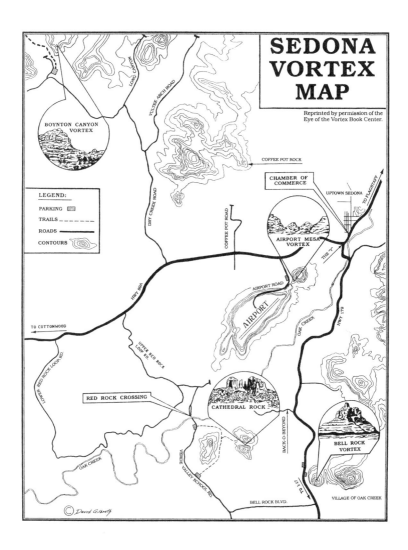

SEDONA VORTEX MAP

Reprinted by permission of the Eye of the Vortex Book Center.

BOYNTON CANYON VORTEX

COFFEE POT ROCK

CHAMBER OF COMMERCE

UPTOWN SEDONA

TO FLAGSTAFF

LONG CANYON

VULTEE ARCH ROAD

DRY CREEK ROAD

COFFEE POT ROAD

AIRPORT MESA VORTEX

THE "Y"

LEGEND:
PARKING
TRAILS
ROADS
CONTOURS

HWY 89A

AIRPORT ROAD

AIRPORT

OAK CREEK

HWY 179

TO COTTONWOOD

UPPER RED ROCK LOOP RD.

LOWER RED ROCK LOOP RD.

RED ROCK CROSSING

CATHEDRAL ROCK

BACK-O-BEYOND

BELL ROCK VORTEX

OAK CREEK

VERDEA

VALLEY SCHOOL RD.

TO I-17

BELL ROCK BLVD.

VILLAGE OF OAK CREEK

© David Gilhooly

CHANNELING

Whatever is going on metaphysically or spiritually in other places is concentrated ten-fold in Sedona. And channeling is no exception. Amongst the new age community here in Sedona which, as I mentioned before, is large, channeling is as common an occurrence as watching football is in Cincinnati.

And so it should be. I believe that channeling - or the use of one's channel to tap into other dimensions of higher energy and clearer reality, is perhaps one of the most valuable tools humanity has at its disposal today. It is for that reason I am devoting more words to it in this chapter with the hope that it will create a better understanding of channeling, which has always been with us, but now is undergoing a resurgence of worldwide proportion.

I am a semi-professional channel and I teach channeling. I taught it in California and in Sedona. My last class in Sedona was scheduled for six weeks and it lasted five and a half months. No one wanted to stop, it was so rewarding. Channeling is one of the most controversial elements in our society today, because of so many variables and religious stigmas that are labeled to it. If you don't believe channeling works - it isn't real. Try it! Not just once, but work at it!

There are two aspects to channeling. One is to allow, through trust, a non-physical cosmic or spiritual entity to borrow, with your consent, your physical body, your systems of expression, to relay vital information to humanity. The other aspect is to use the channel to connect with cosmic sources of information (the universal mind) and using this information to benefit yourself and others in a loving, positive manner.

Everyone has a channel. If you were to view a channel clairvoyantly - it would look like a neon light tube extending from the base of a person's back, through the top of the head, and connecting to Source. Completely developed channels glow very brightly, while one that is not, glows very faintly. There are many individuals walking around today who have fully developed channels and don't even know it. It is a precious tool so often wasted. Often these individuals think they are going crazy because they hear strange voices, see vibrant futuristic visions, or receive involuntary information that is very confusing and perplexing to them. If one has strong, conditioned beliefs about devils and satans, this can be a real dilemma.

CHANNELING

To get good at channeling (clear) it takes a lot of hard work, persistence, diligence and truth of heart. But the rewards are worth all of it. There are those who are natural channels, and can begin almost immediately with great clarity. And I suspect this ability was perfected by them in a past lifetime - Edgar Cayce, Arthur Ford, Jack Pursel (Lazaris) and Jane Roberts (Seth) as examples.

If you wish to experience channeling, do so in a small group of level headed, close friends. Conduct your sessions with no ego and no competition. Ego is absolutely lethal in the metaphysical business. Beginning with a small group (2 to 10 people - "When two or more gather in my name") is the best way because it has built-in balancing devices. To fully explain this last paragraph, and channeling itself in detail, would take volumes. I can only give it superficial treatment here.

A particular caution: if you firmly believe in the existence of Dark Forces - don't try channeling! Forces of darkness as an evil, well organized, ethereal horde of irresistible demons and ghouls bent on taking us over do not exist. Dark Forces as such, exist solely in the collective mind of humanity. And this mythical dark force feeds gleefully on the fear that is fed them. So, if you are into dark forces, you are eventually going to create them and channel them. The human mind is a wondrous instrument - it will create whatever you want.

There are no dark forces, but there does exist low, confused, anxiety ridden astral beings, and a few extra-terrestrials who have questionable motives in mind. Low astrals are human beings who had exceptionally negative lifetime(s) (murderer, power mad, etc.) on this plane and passed on into the astral realm. Ghosts, poltergeists, and doppelgangers fall into this category. In an intelligence and awareness sense, if they were as thick as two planks alive, they are most likely going to be thick as two planks dead. There is NO reason whatsoever to fear low astrals, or extra-terrestrials. If you are AWARE of them, and are secure within yourself, self-loving and know without question your divine sovereignty. You own your own space, it's yours only and that's it!

In my classes, I like to put the astral realms in degrees of 1 to 10. Astrals from the lower astral realm, 6 down to 1, are the ones to be aware of, especially 3 down to 1. But levels 7 to 10 are similar to us in development and generally are intelligent, pleasant and congenial beings.

Channels should bring through only loving, positive, inspiring information. If it is negative in any way, something is wrong. The channel should stop at once and ask for a higher being - Archangel

Michael for example, or any being who is known to be of high spiritual origin.

Sedona has some of the best channels in the world who either reside here or visit here. Its a marvelous learning experience. Channeling is a growing part of our existence now and there is a need to establish a rational understanding of it. Maybe one day there will be special schools that will teach it in classrooms - right up through graduating from grade twelve.

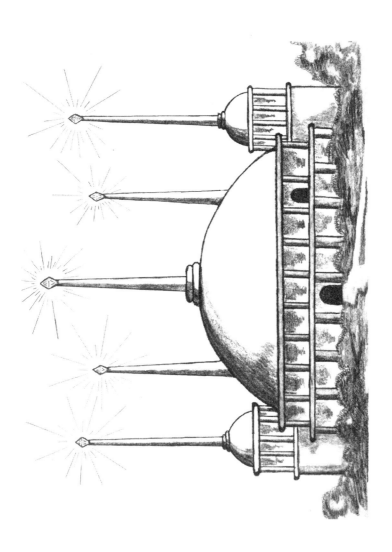

SEDONA: THE RE-EMERGENCE OF LEMURIA

Sedona is presently situated near the area of what was once a great Lemurian city and temple complex. The complex had a central hub located just west of Capitol Butte. It had extensions that radiated out from the center about two miles long each. There were many circular structures which were distributed evenly from the center, to the outer circumference of the city. If viewed from the air, it would resemble three wagon wheels of different diameters placed on top of each other, with the spokes spaced out evenly around the circle.

At regular intervals around the city complex were exquisitely beautiful dome shaped meditation and teaching buildings. These were mostly made of a white stone material. There were enchanting gardens of flowers, and fountains of cascading water. The roofs of some of the rounded structures were semi-transparent and were inlaid with thousands of crystals and gemstones. This allowed for a tremendous expansion of consciousness of anyone meditating or studying under them.

CHAPTER SIX

The Lemurians were beginning to function on a level beyond physical in what might be called the etheric-astral. They were learning to utilize and integrate the most advantageous aspects of both worlds. They had also installed, throughout the temple, energy power spots in which they placed themselves. Here they could project their subconscious (in the etheric/astral) to other dimensions or places where the information and training they sought was more accessible. This later got the Lemurians into trouble, because they were not sufficiently ready to be able to integrate and incorporate the incredibly advanced information and knowledge they had sometimes taken without permission from other systems of evolution. The energy power spots the Lemurians had installed were used to heal as well as transport. The remnants of a few of the more powerful ones remain to this day.

Many of the Lemurian temples were constructed on already existing gridwork leylines of earth energy. The magnificent domes and crystal topped spires even today are still frequently seen by psychics. The ground level of where Lemuria once was is where Sedona now is. Some claim that what is seen is a projection skyward of a buried civilization. It is also believed that enormous crystals are intentionally buried in the rock under Sedona. It is thought by some that these are solely responsible for the spontaneous psychic phenomena that so frequently occurs here. Small pockets of quartz crystals can be found on the surface throughout the red rocks of Sedona, and these no doubt contribute to these exotic energies that are present in the area.

I believe that what is occurring in Sedona on a massive scale is the re-emergence of Lemurian consciousness. It is rising on the etheric planes and will soon merge on the same level where Sedona is now located. This in part explains the absolutely extraordinary visionary and energy effects that so many who come to Sedona experience on the deepest and most profound levels.

This following message was given to me by a discarnate master named Kol-a-sul. "Sedona itself is on the crossroads of an interdimensional pathway of an energy that intersects twelve levels of dimensional reality. This means that one in Sedona with a receptive mind can tune into levels of energy and vital data that far exceed that of another individual in the same place, who limits himself or herself to the comparatively mundane experiencing of what is seen, felt, tasted, and heard with the limited perceptions of the physical apparatus. This type of comprehension expansion can be accomplished in any other locality. But it can be much more readily connected to in Sedona - by the clarity of the energies and the much finer harmonic vibration which currently exists there." (Sedona has very little "big city" type psychic contamination.)

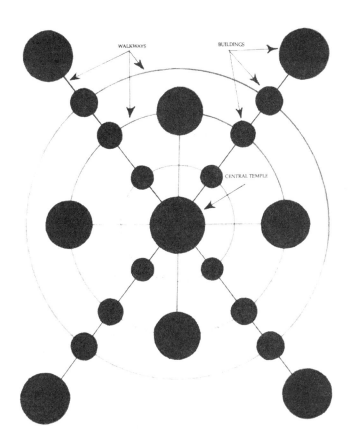

SPACE SHIPS AND PARA-NORMAL OCCURRENCES

Space ship sightings in Sedona are sporadic, usually occurring in a one or two month period during any season of the year. But they can be spectacular. I have spoken at length to a number of people who have had first hand sightings.

Ships are sometimes observed flying in twos or threes in and out of the canyons. One such recent sighting by a Sedona resident was of two UFOs coming out of Fay Canyon at night viewed from a distance of about two miles He said they were both a luminescent red, orange and blue. They flew in formation until about three miles from the canyon, then one went south and the other west. He explained that they were at first traveling at a speed of perhaps 50 miles per hour, then accelerated quickly to about 500 miles per hour. This story is heard with many variations corresponding to the same area at different times. UFO activity seems to be concentrated in this general area.

In one of the more dramatic sightings I know of, two women, a mother and daughter, were driving north to Flagstaff, Arizona, from Sedona on State Route 89A. 89A is a main highway and heavily travelled. About 2:00 PM on a clear, cloudless summer day, the daughter, sitting on the passenger side, looked out the car window and noticed a shiny gray object pacing the automobile about a mile away. The object was just above the tree tops.

This stretch of road is thickly forested by tall ponderosa pines. The two women were able to only get occasional glimpses of the object as it followed along. This situation continued for approximately fifteen minutes, when they suddenly noticed the craft was drawing closer. The approach of the ship continued until it was just a few hundred yards away. They could now see that it was a disc shaped craft with a layered dome on top.

After a continual approach, the ship then positioned itself directly ahead of their car - and less than one hundred yards above the road surface. They told me that at this point there was no mistaking what the object was. A ship. And it was obviously not from this planet.

The forest was particularly tall and dense on this stretch of the road. It was like a high corridor with no ceiling. In front of them the ship began to tilt to a 45 degree angle, and very slowly, it descended lower and lower until it almost touched the car. The two women could clearly observe rows of multi-colored flashing lights which seemed to extend all the way around the base of the craft. The woman driving the car soon found a place to pull over. She brought her car to a sliding stop on the shoulder of the highway. The two then rushed out of the car and looked up in time to see the ship gain altitude, level off, and in moments disappear over the tops of the pine trees. They explained that they at no time experienced any fear at all. In fact, the daughter remarked that there was something strangely familiar and friendly about the ship. They also said that - during the close proximity of the ship - it was remarkably odd that not one car passed either way on the very heavily traveled highway.

In another incident, three prominent local businessmen were hiking in a canyon near Sedona when they all felt an urge to look up. As they turned their gaze skyward, straight above them, and moving at a speed a man could walk, was a gleaming gold disc that made absolutely no sound. They described how the disc filled the sky above them and blotted out the sun. They watched the disc intently for about five minutes, until it glided over the canyon rim, and then out of sight.

CHAPTER SEVEN

My own UFO experience occurred one night while I was camped out in the desert near Secret Canyon. I kept noticing two unusually bright stars that somehow did not look right. I glanced at the stars several more times and assured myself they were just stars and to forget it. Four or five minutes later I looked again. To my absolute astonishment the bright stars were slowly drifting toward one another, and shortly became one light. As I now watched with riveted interest, the one star grew brighter - and brighter - and brighter. And then separated once again into two lights. As I stood watching, the two lights, now moving toward me, drifted directly overhead with no sound whatsoever - no engine sounds - no wind sounds - nothing. They then floated out over the wide expanse of the Verde Valley desert - and then gradually vanished in the distance.

The next UFO incident was told to me by a thirty year old woman who is a very successful publishing executive from New York City. She was in Sedona for the summer writing dialogue for videotapes for her company. One evening after she was finished with her day's work, she decided to walk along Oak Creek in the moonlight. As she walked along, she noticed a bright light on the horizon. The light was moving in her direction, so she continued to watch it. In a short time the light, which she thought was either an airplane head-light or a helicopter searchlight, was drawing very close to where she stood. The light, now of an extreme intensity, was high in front of her, but not directly overhead. She said she still thought it was a searchlight from some sort of aircraft - but there was, strangely, no sound.

As she watched the glaring light, it suddenly switched off. When her eyes finally adjusted to the darkness, what she saw was not a helicopter, but a circular shaped hovering craft. The moon was nearly full, so the metallic superstructure of the ship was in full view with no trees to obstruct her vision. She related to me later that as she watched the craft, she had very odd sensations throughout her body - and that she felt no fear. The ship remained in position for ten to fifteen minutes, then it moved slowly away, and then out of sight over the hills.

As a continuation of this, one week from that night, she was driving her car on a rather isolated stretch of road late at night near Bell Rock. Literally the same exact situation happened again. She said that this time, after she got out of her car, she made an effort to communicate with the craft. She even shouted to it, but got no discernible response other than the craft seemed somehow familiar to her, and she had a deep longing to go with whoever was aboard the ship.

CHAPTER SEVEN

This last UFO incident was told to me by a man whom I will call Jim. Jim was at the time living in Tempe, Arizona, and now resides in Cottonwood, Arizona, which is a few miles from Sedona. He and his friend, who I will call Larry, had an encounter of the third kind - direct contact with space aliens. Jim and Larry had driven up from Tempe to hike for a day in Sycamore Canyon, just southwest of Sedona. Sycamore Canyon is 33 miles long, 1300 feet deep, and half a mile wide in places.

They had driven over a dirt ranch road to a remote trail which led to the bottom of the canyon. They had not watched the time carefully, and after hiking to their destination, found themselves in encroaching darkness on the canyon floor. Having brought along a good flashlight, they were not overly concerned for it was a well defined trail back to where they had parked the pickup truck, at the top of the west side of the canyon.

They had begun the walk back, when they noticed that the canyon rim above them, on the east side, was silhouetted by an intensely bright light. It looked like car headlights just out of sight--only they knew that there was no road on the east rim.

They turned to look more closely and as they did a type of brightly illuminated craft sailed out over the rim and into the canyon. The craft was about

SPACESHIPS AND OCCURRENCES

TOP OF SHIP

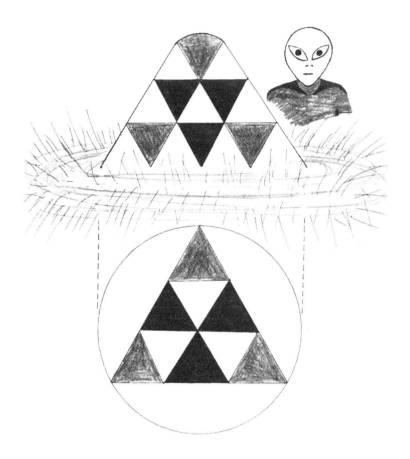

UNDERSIDE

fifty feet in diameter, round at the base but had a pyramid-shaped superstructure Its base was surrounded by a blazingly bright white halo of light. As the craft came closer, the two men could see that the entire surface of the ship was made up of triangles, which were individually either red, white, or green glowing colors. As the ship moved, these triangles would pulse, and the faster the ship moved the faster the triangles would pulse.

The two men had brought with them a powerful set of binoculars and took turns getting a close inspection of the strange vehicle.

Occasionally from the outer rim of the craft, a dazzling red laser-like beam would shoot out, first in one direction, then another.

Tremendously excited about the incredible appearance, Jim began to shine his flashlight in the direction of the ship - in the hope of drawing it even closer. When he switched on his flashlight, the ship retreated back behind the rim from where it had come. Minutes later the ship drifted back out into the canyon a half mile to the south. Jim remarked at the time that the ship seemed to be exhibiting caution in its movements. Wanting it to come closer, he signaled again, using a slow back and forth movement with the flashlight. Exultation overcame him when the craft responded in kind by copying the slow back and forth motion.

At this time, Larry, becoming very nervous and frightened, heavily berated Jim for being so stupid. Jim told me that he felt no fear at all -- just great excitement over what was transpiring. ("Foolish me," he told me at the time of the interview.)

The ship began drifting in their direction and at the same time descending lower, to half the height of the canyon wall -- where it stopped. Jim was closely watching the ship through the binoculars when a red dot appeared on the right lens of the binoculars. Immediately after that, his head was suddenly engulfed in a billowing red shaft of light which followed the smaller red laser-like beam. He said it "was like getting kicked in the head by an electronic mule."

The next thing Jim remembered was his friend Larry, half pulling him and half dragging him, shouting "Let's get out of here, let's get out of here!!" Jim then lost all memory of what happened at that point. He said the next thing he knew it was pitch dark and they were on flat ground next to Larry's pickup truck. He didn't know how they had gotten there.

Jim distantly asked Larry, "What happened? What happened to us?" Larry responded quickly in high agitation, "I don't want to talk about it! You should never ask me! I won't ever tell you! Forget it!"

Over the next four days Jim experienced long bouts of total amnesia and unusual combative behavior.

Years later Jim ran into Larry one day and asked if he could now explain what had happened to them. Larry was by then relaxed about the event and could only say for certain, now, was that he remembered the ship taking off from the ground near them on the floor of the canyon - and that was it.

Jim to this day avoids reading anything about UFO encounters in books, magazines and newspapers.

An interesting addition to this account occurred one day a few years after the Sycamore Canyon experience. Jim, now living in Cottonwood, was driving with his wife in the area of Bell Rock. They were proceeding north and two cars, close together, were approaching from the opposite direction. The car in the rear suddenly pulled out to pass. It was an imminent, unavoidable, head on, high speed collision.

Then something unusual happened. The car that remained in the driving lane in an instant changed into a vertical shape - like a tall, thick line - Jim said it was "like something out of a Disney cartoon." The car that was going to hit them stretched out horizontally until it was only a few feet wide. Both "cars" moved to the left and flew by them. He relates that he and his wife were in such a state of shock that they drove three miles before they could pull over and talk about it.

On this same stretch of road, near Bell Rock, a car with five adults in it had an unusual visitor. The car in which they were riding was a luxury model and the sun roof was drawn back. One of the passengers looked up, and pacing the car, just above the open sun roof, was an orange sphere the size of a large beach ball. Some of the passengers, especially the driver, got quite nervous. The sphere followed along with them for a few minutes and then sped away into the distance.

As a last word on unusual phenomena in Sedona I will mention a lady I know quite well. She owns a most unusual house surrounded by much open land. She has had many extraterrestrial visitors. They seem to have come with the property along with the expansive house she had built on the land. It has been suggested that the design of the house was supplied by ETs for some purpose known only to them. They also seem to be guarding the property - woe to the first burglar who tries to break into her house.

Human-looking beings in what might be termed space dress have been seen by many visitors to her home - and some beings that might fall into the spirit category (both occurrences surprisingly common in Sedona). Some of the witnesses to these appearances were construction workers who had little or no beliefs about visitors from outer space.

One of the most memorable sightings at her house happened late one night. Due to a lack of communication, a man and wife who were to meet at her house arrived, not having gotten the message that the function that they had come for had been canceled and no one was home. The house was dark as all the lights were turned off. But they saw a light glowing at the rear of the house and thought they could see someone moving around. They thought everyone was out on the patio. They decided to walk around to the back through the bushes for they concluded that someone had forgotten to leave the outside lights on. They got quite a shock as they made their way around to the rear of the house.

As they rounded a corner of the building, they saw a line of luminous beings gliding down a staircase where there was no stairway. The light these beings gave off lit up the whole back yard. The couple beat a very hasty retreat back to their car.

SPACESHIPS AND OCCURRENCES

Author's Note:

It's interesting that the government generally disavows or ridicules the existence of UFOs - and related non-earth beings and and their vehicles. Despite this policy, we have the testimony of individuals such as astronaut Colonel Gordon Cooper, Lt. Colonel Coyne, General Nathan Twining, J. Edgar Hoover, Senator Barry Goldwater, President Jimmy Carter, and Lt. Colonel Wendelle Stevens of sightings or first hand knowledge of extraterrestrial vehicles and their occupants.

It is even more interesting to note that there is a federal law on the books against U.S. Citizens interacting with extraterrestrial space aliens or their vehicles; to the extent that an individual could be siezed and held under armed guard, without court hearing, for an indefinite period. Although to my knowledge this law has not been used, yet, - it exists. It is Title 14, Section 1211 of the Code of Federal Regulations, adopted July 16, 1969.

SEDONA AND THE DAYS AHEAD

Sedona is, metaphysically, a compendium. It is a condensed summary of what is going on in the rest of the world. Sedona is not by itself exclusively unique, for there are other places where there are similar concentrations of futuristic energies and occurrences. But Sedona is a special place due to the unique thinness of the "veil" between our world and the world "on the other side." The other side denotes an availability of dimensions, universes, unspeakably powerful energies, and non-human beings visible and invisible. This realm is totally and readily accessible by all - now - everywhere.

The future is actualizing now in Sedona in part by a gathering of some of the most serious, most dedicated, most conscious (awake) individuals on the planet. They are being called here from everywhere. Perhaps soon we will know the exact reason why. Sedona is, and has been, the proving ground for emerging abilities and potentialities, and I suspect that it will in a short time be the world center for the implementation of the "New Age". The true beginning of the rational exploration of the truth of "ALL THAT IS".

SEDONA AND THE DAYS AHEAD

There are two areas involving humanity which I believe demand our complete attention without further delay, and they are: (1) the absolutely incredible recent rise in the frequency of alien being and space ship interactions with humanity worldwide. We need to recognize the reality that these entities exist and establish some kind of working, beneficial relationship with these beings, or at least one race, as soon as safely possible. The ignorance is on our side, not theirs.

(2) We need to utilize, fully, emerging powers of creation which we possess, and that the majority of mankind are either ignoring, or are refusing to believe in its existence. These powers of creation and the pressure of realization within our consciousness is growing to the exploding point. This pleading inner rise in awareness needs to be recognized and acknowledged, and thus released into positive manifestation. Sedona is, I think in a fashion, a triggering point, a flashpoint in consciousness for these rising, emerging probabilities - which will then ignite the mass consciousness of receptive humanity.

Mankind is on the threshold of a change which may only occur once in the evolution of a race such as ours. Its coming has many interpretations depending on the point of view. But most would agree, no matter what their religious or spiritual beliefs are, that a great change is in the air - and long overdue.

Have we so imbedded ourselves in a stagnant, outdated pattern of reality that we are overlooking a greater, more infinitely beneficial reality that transcends anything we could imagine? There is a very real possibility that this coming great transition point could be lost merely because of a willful ignorance by a majority of humanity. A refusing to accept that there is "something" emerging that is more powerful than we are - but yet at the same time something that we ourselves have set in motion through the Divine Forces that operate under these laws. And what do we need to do to prepare for this event? The answer lies in simplicity - simply open, expand to, and lovingly receive what we have created - and what is being compassionately managed by forces beyond our present understanding.

The time has come to allow unconditional love, to allow our hearts and intuition to chart the course. It has never failed.

This is all, fundamentally, a preview of what humanity on a grand scale will soon be dealing with. Dealing with as the energies and probabilities of a new era in human experiencing arrives into our reality. That time is not in the hazy future - it is now. With all its freedom, joyous anticipation, excitement and opportunity. It is now.

On a Sedona Energy Spring

READER'S COMMENTS

The following commentaries are by individuals I asked to give their views on Sedona, the book, or a metaphysical experience they have had that directly relates to Sedona. I extend warmest thanks to these people who graciously allowed me to print their names and who honestly and openly expressed what was on their hearts and minds.

Sedona contains insights and energies which are enlightening and expanding to heart, mind and soul. I shall return again and again.

Helmut Hoehl
Alberta, Canada

As one who is intimately aware of the many factors of the Sedona experience, I applaud this guidepost book for those who might be looking toward Sedona as their next residence and experience. The wisdom and frankness, as well as the advice related to interacting with the environment and beings resident here, of course apply to all no matter what the location.

John Graham
Sedona

A magical, subtle energy does pervade all of Sedona.

It has been said that every red rock formation in Sedona is an energy source/transmitter, and that there are countless, or at least hundreds, of vortexes, or energy springs as Tom explains.

READER'S COMMENTS

Other areas that have particularly gotten my attention are Schnebly Hill, Long Canyon, Fay Canyon, and the trail up the West Fork of Oak Creek Canyon - one of extraordinary beauty. It is in West Fork that there is supposed to be a portal to the inner earth - and I believe that the Lord Michael is giving us this information in truth (through channelings) for our understanding and in some cases future use.

Tom Dongo's "Mysteries of Sedona" contains more of the esoteric truths in my opinion than anything printed to date on Sedona. I vouch for his spiritual integrity, clairvoyant gifts, and this contribution to the new wave of Sedona literature as people the world over discover this new spiritual capital.

Richard Huffer
Sedona

The Mysteries of Sedona: a very informal and appropriate explanation of Sedona's role in the worldwide change of awareness.

R. Nelson
Minnesota

Sedona is like a portal - an opening into the memory of who we are . . . THE GREAT RIVER . . .which contains the source of all creation and thought.

P.R.H.
Sedona

I very much enjoyed this book. My only regret is that it's not longer. Sedona truly sparkles with aliveness. I really loved my short visit and I'm sure I'll make a return trip sometime. Just those few short days had a profound effect on me. How wonderful it must be to live there. Reading "Mysteries of Sedona" brought back for me some of that Sedona energy, and the night that I slept in the vortex I had some of the most intensely wonderful dreams I've had in a very long time.

I agree with you when you say that all of Boynton Canyon is an energy spring. I hiked back into the canyon very late one night and experienced a very unusual cool breeze which seemed to come from the back of the canyon. This breeze had an edge to it, although not hostile, and an intensity that would have made sleeping very difficult if not impossible. All of my senses were very much awake. Curiously, this breeze was felt very little once I crossed over the dry creek bed and approached the resort area on my way out of the canyon. This was also very interesting for me, because this dry creek bed was also where you told us that the energy starts increasing as one walks back into the canyon.

Michael Marshall
Oregon

A personal event I would like to mention is my experience with the "thinning veil" in Sedona. Shortly after moving to Sedona, I awoke one night and sat up in bed staring at the stars - suddenly I realized I was hearing a chorus of voices, no words, just incredible harmonies. It was the most beautiful music. I immediately thought of angels singing, for that is what it sounded like. I have not again heard the music since that night, but I have met several others who have had the same experience.

READER'S COMMENTS

Since my first visit to Sedona on my honeymoon, my husband and I knew this would be our home, although at that time we knew nothing about the specialness of Sedona. By the way, we were also drawn here from the East Coast.

I am a professional artist and my artwork has changed dramatically from being in Sedona. I was supercharged with energy and creativity. My senses were heightened and after living here for awhile, the process just continues to expand and unfold. One does not remain stagnant in Sedona. You either grow - or move somewhere else.

Maru Cronin
Sedona

I am certain that the evolution of mankind is an ever developing process, but acting in our daily life schedules keeps us sometimes grounded in a rather narrow physical and mental awareness. Reality, I think, is wider that the effort of our own thinking.

In every second we are surrounded by the intelligences and consciousnesses of the entire universe. By understanding its principles we are able to understand cosmic laws - and this perhaps is our next step in understanding the process of ourselves, and the world we live in.

This book will give you some hints on how to go, and how to accomplish reality in your life. Thomas Dongo gives you an intellectual idea of what mankind truly will accomplish, and that we are standing at the threshold of new voyages of discovery.

Kjell Eidendahl
Sweden

READER'S COMMENTS

I am one who feels good about this kind of metaphysical information being brought out about the Sedona area.

We all have had experiences which elicit the "wows" and the unexplained. I wish to share how I came to be drawn to Sedona from my home in California.

While sleeping one night I heard the word "Sedona, Sedona, Sedona," over and over and over. Upon awakening I thought to myself, "Oh! I have been given a name change!" That very day a friend returned from vacation and brought me a magazine about Arizona. I opened it and read, "Sedona, Arizona." Through tear-filled eyes I looked at a picture of Cathedral Rock and I knew it was the red rock mountain I had seen in my dreams for years.

Not long after - keeping my own name - I moved to Sedona: to continue my journey.

Donna Marie Norman
Sedona

This was definitely one of the most enjoyable books I have ever read. It even has a few laughs, and yet, the material was very real and important to me. I have been to Sedona five times in ten months, and am planning another visit in a month or so! I can't seem to stay away from the place.

I have spent four nights camping out around Sedona and have had some interesting experiences with what I felt to be extraterrestrials. Also, I must say, I look forward to more of them.

READER'S COMMENTS

Perhaps this is a part of what draws me to Sedona, then perhaps it is "merely" that I feel so alive and clear when I visit there.

Jan Lehn
Oregon

One year has now passed since the Harmonic Convergence of 1987. At that time I was living in Minnesota and was very entrenched in the materialistic world, almost totally unaware of my own spirituality - and the New Age Movement. We had begun to look at the way we were living and decided that there just had to be a better way.

My wife and I left jobs, families, friends; sold out and moved from Minnesota to Portland, Oregon, where we stayed a total of two and one half months. After four weeks in Portland we visited Sedona with a tour group from Oregon. Upon our return to Portland, it was only a short time before we packed up a trailer with our belongings and moved to Sedona. The changes came so rapidly that I now look back in wonderment at the changes that we've manifested so quickly. Good changes.

During our initial visit to Sedona the first person we met was Tom Dongo. It is truthfully our feeling that Tom has far more understanding of the energy areas, or vortexes if you will, than any other source we have read or heard in the eight months we have lived in Sedona. Tom has shared with us information that the average seeker of the light coming to Sedona never becomes exposed to.

READER'S COMMENTS

If one coming to Sedona in search of truth and knowledge does not get the opportunity to meet Tom, and hear him channel, we believe that they have truly missed a chance of a lifetime. This book is by far the best I have ever read on Sedona.

John and Marybeth Roberts
Sedona

I live in Oregon and love it there. But a year ago I first experienced Sedona - and I have changed.

My experience in Sedona was one of clearing, healing, and enchantment. Because of the Sedona energies, I met myself. I love the cactus, the red rocks, the majestic land, and the people. Sedona opened my heart and allowed me to face my fears - and assisted me to release them. In a way, I am myself now a Sedonan.

When I travel to Sedona, I am going home. Each trip is a different experience in itself. If you want to meet yourself and go home, go to Sedona. It will welcome you. It is calling you, and waiting for you. You will either love yourself and Sedona - or you will run away.

Diane Warren
Oregon

Diane Warren is a clear channel who channels a master named Ramas. This is an excerpt from a May, 1988 session:

RAMAS: "Sedona is very much a light center. It is the ancient land of Lemuria. Lemuria was land in your past where gods came and they brought their light and they incarnated upon this plane, and they bred with the entities upon this plane. In your history darkness came as man began to go into the process of what you call implosion. And the gods left, and the entities who were upon this plane graduated to Atlantis and the darkness took over. And the darkness manifested greatly in Atlantis with the destruction of a continent.

Now that place that is Sedona is the ancient land of Lemuria. There is much energy there - there is much wisdom, much holiness and much purity; and there are entities there who are grand receptacles of the light. The earth itself is now releasing this light that is stored in the actual physicalness of the plane. Many entities come to this place. And when they come a release of the light within them occurs. And it allows us to give, to send, and to trigger more light to this place Sedona. Now, you see it is a very powerful spot on your planet. When entities go to Sedona and the light is being released within them, they then often go back to their places of origin and they bring a wondrous stream of light with them. So that an actual stream of light occurs. And a connection is made. And each time a trip to Sedona - more light - this stream of light - is strengthened and broadened.. . . ."

Ramas/Diane Warren

"The Mysteries of Sedona" provides entertaining and informative reading about Sedona's unique qualities which will give visitors and locals alike some clues and fresh ideas to the vortexes and special energies of our area. I found myself relating to one UFO experience described by the author. One evening, a friend and I drove out to the Fay Canyon area to look at the stars without the interference of the city's lights. It was an incrediby clear night, the stars were brilliant. No sooner had we gotten out of the car and looked upward than we saw what at first we thought was a falling star, only this star was falling within the earth's atmosphere and very close to where we were. As it came closer, we noticed the red, white and blue lights. When it was right above us, it divided into two objects which jetted away from each other with incredible silence and speed - one shooting upwards towards the northwest, the other right over us to the northeast. And it was gone. It happened so quickly, ° yet is vividly ingrained in my mind. This was in late February, 1987 at about 11:30 P.M. How exciting!

This book is excellent reading. Enjoy. Relate and come to some new understandings about this special place called Sedona.

Jeana Pinyan
Sedona

You've treated Sedona like a delicious, rich cheesecake - and given us only a thin slice! I want more! Indeed.

Sedona certainly gave a lively boost to my own emotional/spiritual process. Going to Sedona and sleeping out under the stars in a vortex helped me to let go of the great block of fear that I had created and carried with me for such a long time. Sedona acted as the turning point or, as you suggested in the book, as a great triggering device in breaking up this deadening gridlock of energy within me.

READER'S COMMENTS

We can call upon the energy of Sedona much as we may call upon the knowledge and love of the light beings that we channel, and use this energy as a wonderful divine tool that allows us to straightaway SEE and FEEL the places that need healing within us. Indeed, as you say, Sedona does feel like an intense energy spring of grace and light. Naturally, how we receive this sacred gift depends upon our focus, our deepest intentions and how willingly and lovingly we allow this knowledge into our heart of hearts.

Don Cauble
Oregon

In the last four years, Sedona has provided for me a safe and nurturing environment of allowance and encouragement to lift my own "veils." My experience in Sedona has been one of being at home on planet earth.

It seems that the purity and clarity of energies here calls forth the EXPRESSION of one's own clarity and purity of heart and soul. Those with many unresolved (unloved?) energies and issues within their beings, have oftentimes found this intensification here to be overwhelming and uncomfortable.

I think that because of the emerging Sedona energies, many of us have been drawn back to a very ancient familiar home.

Calida
Sedona

Sedona, great center of light, has been a great assistance on my path. On my first trip to Sedona I felt that I had entered a new dimension. For the first time in my life I

READER'S COMMENTS

became aware of new realities and of dimensions beyond the third dimensional realities in which our lives have been traditionally grounded. That trip was an opener for me - an eye-opener, a mind-opener, a heart-opener. On my second trip some difficulties I was in the process of moving through were greatly intensified and I was thereby able to move through them in a much shorter time than had I not gone to Sedona. I plan to travel to Sedona many times to process and to heal and to experience this sacred and holy place.

Susan D. Snead
Oregon

One time when Janet and I were together at Bell Rock, she saw the members of the angelic kingdom using the vortex there. The vortex looked like a green shimmering crystal and the angels would come and dip into it (for the energy, I assume) and go off with it. They were very busy and didn't seem to notice anything or anyone else. We assumed that this is the way they get some of the energy for the earth building and repairing projects that they do for humanity and the earth.

Janet McClure and Lillian Harben,
co-founders of the Tibetan
Foundation, Phoenix

CLIMATE

Sedona's weather is typical high desert. Sedona's elevation is 4300 feet which rises abruptly to 7000 feet to the nearby Mogollon Rim. During the months of June, July and August, it is very hot, usually around 100 degrees daily, dropping to 60 or 70 degrees at night. Hikers should carry ample drinking water and wear head covering at all times. July and August are the Monsoon months, with spectacular electrical storms, late afternoon rain deluges and awe-inspiring sunsets. September, October, and November are generally dry, but with the possibility of flash flood rains.

Mid-day temperatures are in the low 90's September to the 70's in November. December, January, February, March, April, and May temperatures can range from daytime 50-80's to low twenties at night. Storms of rain and snow can appear quickly so extra gear is needed in the backcountry. Daytime, the winter months are the most delightful of the year - ideal for outdoor activities. Major snow storms average three a winter and the snow usually is melted after two or three days. Mid-winter nights can be cold with temperatures sometimes in the teens with brisk winds.

RATTLESNAKES

No comprehensive writing about Sedona would be complete without some mention of rattlesnakes. I have discovered that it is on every hiker's mind, and that surprisingly little is available in the form of printed information on rattlesnakes - and what to do about them. I think that those who are engaged in tourism would rather hope that no one brings up the subject, and that somehow it will all go away by itself.

It has been a curious experience observing visitors to Sedona who arrive here from non-rattlesnake areas of the country. Some think that there is a rattlesnake as big as an Amazon boa constrictor (they grow up to 30 feet long) lying in ambush, just for them, behind every rock, tree, and cactus...and act according to that belief. At times it could have been a comical situation had not the person on snake alert been so serious about it all - and not at all receptive to chuckles from a local hiker.

There is a great deal of misconception about rattlesnakes, usually garnered from an exaggerated account through a book that was read, or poor advice from a well-meaning friend.

RATTLESNAKES

During the winter months in Sedona there is no danger from snakes, because they are hibernating. So during that time you can go anywhere you want to with peace of mind. Even in the summer months here it is extremely rare to cross paths with a rattlesnake. And if and when you do, they are very interesting creatures to observe - that is if you see them first - if you don't it can be quite a thrill. I would say that as a conservative average estimate, if a person hiked on the desert and canyon trails around Sedona three days a week all through the snake season, they MIGHT see two or three rattlesnakes during that time. I have spoken to Sedona residents who have lived here for five years or more and have never seen a rattlesnake.

Many of the actual rattlesnake bites in Arizona were, and are, to persons that were antagonizing the snake - adolescent males being macho, etc. - and half of those bites were "dry bites". The snake does not want to waste venom on something it cannot eat. It would prefer to save its venom for its usual food, small animals - mice, etc. But it should be remembered that in the Sedona area live some of the most formidable snakes on the planet; among them are timber rattlers, coral snakes, green mohaves and diamondbacks. However, even the biggest,stupidest rattlesnake knows it can't eat a hiker, and could easily be killed by a hiker, so it would much rather avoid a confrontation. Rattlesnakes are great bluffers and simply want to be left alone to go about their business - they have to make a living too. Rattlesnakes do not attack - they defend themselves.

I am not belittling the danger from rattlesnakes because potentially they are decidedly dangerous creatures - especially the larger ones. But again, the possibility of even seeing one is remarkably rare.

The precautions, and this goes for centipedes and scorpions too, are to watch where you put your hands and feet, where you sit. Snakes, scorpions and centipedes hide in and under rocks and deadwood. If you can avoid it, don't sleep in a sleeping bag on bare ground - sleep in a tent. These desert creatures are very active at night. If you wish, wear heavy leggings or baggy pants, most snake bites are to the lower legs. Basically it comes down to common sense - keep your eyes open, LOOK! Look where you are and look where you are going. Besides, after walking into a cactus or two you will become very careful anyway - it's the way of the desert. Many will attest that desert living is good living indeed, and I wouldn't trade it for anything. Most lifetime residents of the desert have never had an unpleasant encounter with the desert's poisonous dwellers.

In reference to over-the-counter snake bite kits it is generally advised now that, unless you are in a remote area and have no choice, snake bite kits can do more damage than good. This is due to many cases of improper use by novices. The current recommendation is, if bit, to go straight to the nearest hospital. Even a serious bite by a large snake to a healthy person in the prime years is seldom fatal. Those at greatest risk are toddlers and the elderly.

My last tip on rattlesnakes is that if you own a dog, and you know for certain that there are rattlers around - leave the dog at the motel or in the car. If you want to see a rattlesnake get really excited, have your dog run by one. The snake thinks the dog is a coyote, and coyotes sometimes eat rattlesnakes.

West Sedona

Red Rock Crossing

AFTERWORD

There have been times when clairvoyantly I have encountered something which might, due to its bizarreness, border on the limits of the mind's ability to accept the strangeness of such a sighting. I will then (if I feel it is important enough) call upon the talents of others who are also recognized clairvoyants. I do this to either validate the sighting or refute the experience completely. Such is that of the "Rock People."

There is a very, very fine line between a projection or fantasy...and reality. The great trick is to learn the difference between what is real in etheric and physical/etheric terms, and what is perhaps a psychic projection of yours, mine, or someone else's.

At the outset I wondered if I were merely imagining the rock people - an illusion. Over a period of several months, I asked at different times a half-dozen known psychics to accompany me to the area where I had first encountered these beings. In this instance the confirmation of what I had found was stunning - to put it mildly. I did not tell the psychics what to expect, nor did I let them read my mind pictures. Not only did each validate the existence of the rock people, but each contributed some fascinating information through their own particular abilities.

It is my hope that the ultimate result of this book will be to make people think, and consider realms of existence they might not normally be accustomed to - or aware of.

This book has quickly gone into its second printing - and has turned out to be highly popular and successful, much to my relief.

May you, with Love and Joy, have the greatest possible success in your search for spiritual enlightenment.

Tom Dongo

ABOUT THE AUTHOR

The author is an internationally published writer. This book is based on an article which appeared in the 1988 November-December issue of Magazine 2000, Europe's largest metaphysical magazine.

RELATED PUBLICATIONS

"An Overview of the Geophysical Aspects of Vortexes," by Alsgoud Sprinke, RMA Light Press, P.O. Box 1292, Sedona, AZ 86336.

"Sedona: Psychic Energy Vortexes," by Dick Sutphen, Valley of the Sun Publishing, Box 38, Malibu, CA 90265.

Tapes on Inner Earth, UFO Contacts, etc., by Virgil (Posty) Armstrong, P.O. Box 20174, Village of Oak Creek, AZ 86341.

"The Sedona Vortex Experience," by Barclay and Johansen, Sunlight Productions, P.O. Box 1300, Sedona, AZ 86336.

Tape on Sedona Vortexes, by Page Bryant, 130 Pinto Lane, Sedona, AZ 86336.

If you found *The Mysteries of Sedona* to be interesting and intriguing, then highly recommended is the second book in the **Mysteries of Sedona Series,** *The Mysteries of Sedona, Book Two: The Alien Tide.*

The Alien Tide is the result of three years of serious research and over one hundred interviews with those who have had mysterious and mystical experiences in and around Sedona, Arizona.

> *"I really enjoyed The Alien Tide. I couldn't put it down. Started reading it at midnight and finished it at 4 a.m."*
>
> **Teddy Haggarty**
> **Film Director**

ORDERING BOOKS BY TOM DONGO

_____autographed copies of *The Mysteries of Sedona* (@ $6.95 ea.) $ _____

_____autographed copies of *The Mysteries of Sedona, Book Two:* **The Alien Tide** (@ $7.95 ea.) $ _____

Postage & Handling: ($2 first book, $1 ea. thereafter.) $ _____

TOTAL: $ _____

(For orders outside the U.S., please write for rates.)

Name _____

Address _____

_____

Send check or money order to:
Mysteries of Sedona
P.O. Box 2571
Sedona, AZ 86336

NOTES

NOTES

NOTES